OUR Christmas BOOK

by Jane Belk Moncure
illustrated by Krystyna Stasiak and
Gwen Connelly

THE CHILD'S WORLD

ELGIN, ILLINOIS 60120

Art Credits:
Pages 9, 13, 14, 15, 16, 18, 21, 22, 26,
and 29 by Krystyna Stasiak.

Pages 4, 5, 6, 7, 8, 10, 11, 12, 17, 19, 23,
25, 27, 28, 30, 31, and 32 by Gwen Connelly.

Distributed by Childrens Press, 1224 West Van Buren Street, Chicago, Illinois 60607.

Library of Congress Cataloging in Publication Data

Moncure, Jane Belk.
  Our Christmas book.

  (A Special-day book)
  Summary: Suggests activities for celebrating
Christmas in the classroom by following members of a
class as they make gifts, puppets,
piñatas, and small trees, decorate a big tree, and
write their own stories.
    1. Christmas decorations—Juvenile literature.
2. Handicraft—Juvenile literature. [1. Christmas
decorations.   2. Handicraft]   I. Stasiak, Krystyna, ill.
II. Connelly, Gwen, ill.   III. Title.   IV. Series.
TT900.C4M66   1986   745.594′1   85-29132
ISBN 0-89565-341-9

    4 5 6 7 8 9 10 11 12 R 95 94 93 92 91 90 89

OUR Christmas BOOK

This book is about how we celebrated Christmas in our class. You will have more ideas in your class.

One day Miss Berry asked, "How can we bring Christmas into our room?"

Joe said, "Let's build a Christmas toy store." So we did.

We drew pictures of toys. We made
play money. Then we opened the toy
store. We took turns being customers.

holly

bow

Merry Christmas

Our Holiday

gift

wreath

tree

candles

stocking

Word Sleigh

Santa

star

snowman

sleigh

reindeer

Miss Berry made a big paper sleigh. We filled it with holiday words. Our holiday word sleigh covered the whole wall.

We used lots of the holiday words in
Christmas stories and poems. Miss Berry
helped us write them. Each of us put
his story or poem in a book. And Miss
Berry read the books to the class.

Merry Christmas

We are authors.
Read our books.

The Tree by Kim

Santa Claus by Joe

The Special Star by Alicia

My Stocking by Eric

THE CHRISTMAS TREE by Joel

The Lost Reindeer by Betsy

A Snowman by Sue

"Now we have a library of books in
our room," said Beth.

Before long, Miss Berry brought a real Christmas tree to school. Stevie said, "Now our room smells like Christmas."

We decorated our tree with gifts from other trees. We painted pine cones, seeds, and dried leaves. We stuffed apples and oranges with cloves. We put red ribbons on some gifts. Then we put strings of popcorn and cranberries around the tree. The whole room smelled spicy.

We sat around the Christmas tree.
Miss Berry told us a story, using a
paper Christmas tree which became
three trees. Then we each made a
tree, so we could tell the story to
somebody else. I will tell it to you.

9" paper, folded to 4½"

12"

fold

cut here

Bear's Tree

5" Squirrel's Tree

cut

Bear's Tree

2" Mouse's Tree

cut

Squirrel's Tree

HOW LITTLE BEAR SHARED

Little Bear had a big Christmas tree.
But poor Little Squirrel had none.

So. . .Little Bear shared.
He cut off part of his big tree and
gave it to Little Squirrel.

Then Little Squirrel had a middle-sized
tree. But poor Little Mouse had none.

So. . .Little Squirrel shared.
He cut off the top of his middle-
sized tree and gave it to Little Mouse.

Then Little Mouse had a little tree.
"Just right for me," said Little Mouse.
And he put the tree in his mouse house.

So all three had Christmas trees—
all because Little Bear shared.

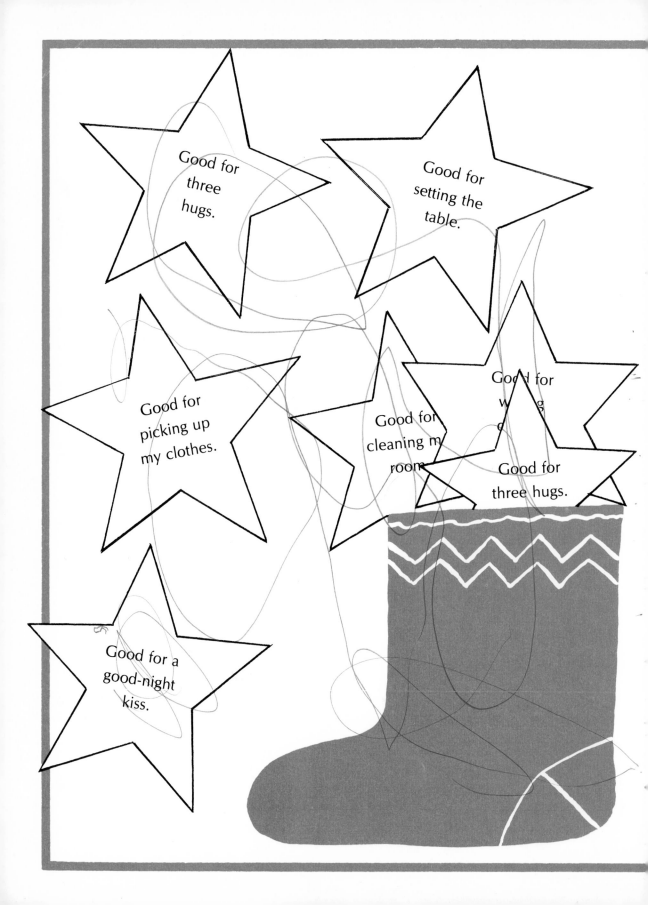

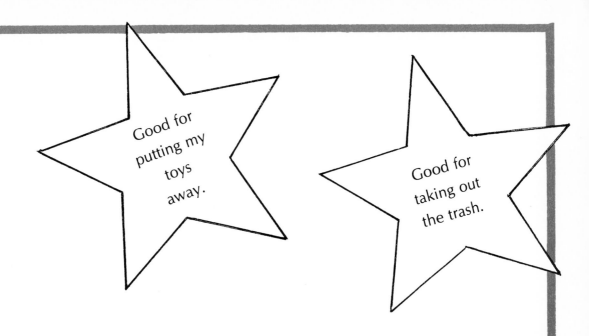

Good for putting my toys away.

Good for taking out the trash.

"Little Bear shared what he had," said Miss Berry. "You can share at Christmas too. You have special gifts you can share."

She gave each of us a bunch of colored stars. On each star we wrote something special we could do.

We stuffed our star gifts into paper stockings to take home for Christmas.

"Wow! Will my mom be surprised!" said Joe.

"Let's make jingle-tingle, rhyming bells," said Miss Berry one morning.

We cut out bell shapes. We wrote words that rhymed on them. Then we played a game. We mixed the bells. Then we took turns matching the words that rhymed— two by two.

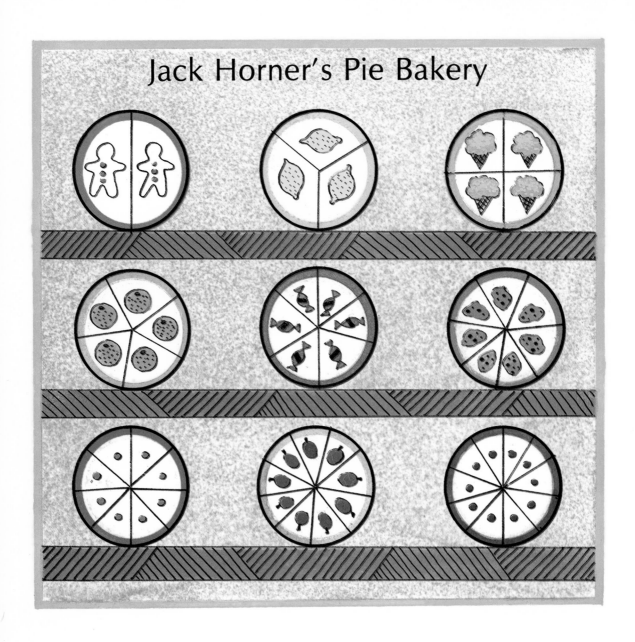

Jack Horner's Pie Bakery

One day, Mark said, "Let's turn our
toy store into a Christmas bakery."
So we made paper-plate pies. We cut
the pies into different-sized slices.

three-piece
pie

five-piece
pie

Jack Horner's
Pie Bakery

"Let's mix and match our pies," said
Mark. Sometimes it took many slices
to make one pie.

We made Christmas "pies" for the birds too. Some of us stuffed pine cones with peanut butter, raisins, birdseed, and cornmeal. Some of us washed and dried milk cartons. Miss Berry helped us cut holes in them. Then we put some "pie" inside each carton.

Miss Berry put strings on the cartons. Then we hung the "pies" outside.

"Now the birds can have Christmas
'pie,' and not get wet," Andy said.

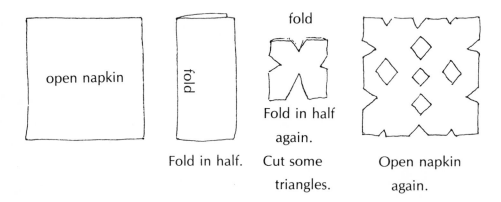

open napkin

fold

Fold in half.

fold

Fold in half
again.

Cut some
triangles.

Open napkin
again.

The next day it snowed. So we
made paper-napkin snowflakes. We
danced as snowflake fairies and
Christmas elves.

When Miss Berry said, ''The sun is
getting hot,'' we melted. . . slowly. . .
all the way to the floor.

Next, we played a snowflake game. There were groups of three people all around the room. Two were a Christmas tree. One was a snowflake. There was one extra snowflake, Julie, looking for a tree.

Miss Berry said, ''Run, little snowflakes; one, two, three. Run and find a new Christmas tree.''

All the snowflakes ran to new trees. Julie found one. Andy became the extra snowflake.

One afternoon, Mary made a talking
toy robot. She made it from a paper
bag. Then she gave a puppet show.

We all wanted to make talking toy puppets. So we did.

What do you think these puppets said?

Alicia made some snowmen finger puppets. She said a poem to the class. We
wanted to say it too. So Miss Berry wrote
it on the chalkboard.

5

Five little snowmen knocked on my door.
One came inside to play.
And that left. . .

4

Four little snowmen climbed a holly tree.
One climbed down and rolled away.
And that left. . .

3

Three little snowmen went to the zoo.
One rode away on a polar bear.
And that left. . .

2

Two little snowmen went skiing. Oh,
    what fun!
One tumbled down a hill.
And that left. . .

1

One little snowman went for a run.
The morning sun melted him.
And that left. . .

0

Guess what was hanging in our
room just before Christmas vacation?
It was a real piñata from Mexico.

"I could make a piñata," said Alicia.
Miss Berry said we all could. So we
did. We made them from lunch bags.

"Tomorrow we will open our big piñata," said Miss Berry.

"Does it have candy in it?" asked Beth.

"Yes," said Miss Berry. "And you can put some of it in your piñatas before you take them home."

The next day Beth said, "Close your
eyes for this surprise, Miss Berry."

She gave Teacher a star and a big
hug. "This hug is my Christmas star
gift just for you," Beth said.